ARKANSAS

by Patricia Lantier

GARETH**STEVENS**

PUBLISHING

A Member of the WRC Media Family of Companies

Please visit our web site at: www.garethstevens.com
For a free color catalog describing Gareth Stevens Publishing's
list of high-quality books and multimedia programs, call
1-800-542-2595 (USA) or 1-800-387-3178 (Canada).
Gareth Stevens Publishing's fax: (414) 332-3567.

Library of Congress Cataloging-in-Publication Data

Lantier, Patricia, 1952-
    Arkansas / Patricia Lantier.
        p. cm. — (Portraits of the states)
    Includes bibliographical references and index.
    ISBN 0-8368-4661-3 (lib. bdg.)
    ISBN 0-8368-4680-X (softcover)
    1. Arkansas—Juvenile literature. I. Title. II. Series.
  F411.3.L36   2006
  976.7—dc22   2005054328

This edition first published in 2006 by
Gareth Stevens Publishing
A Member of the WRC Media Family of Companies
330 West Olive Street, Suite 100
Milwaukee, WI 53212 USA

This edition copyright © 2006 by Gareth Stevens, Inc.

Editorial direction: Mark J. Sachner
Project manager: Jonatha A. Brown
Editor: Catherine Gardner
Art direction and design: Tammy West
Picture research: Diane Laska-Swanke
Indexer: Walter Kronenberg
Production: Jessica Morris and Robert Kraus

Picture credits: Cover, pp. 15, 20, 24, 26, 27 © John Elk III; p. 4 Hot Springs
Convention & Visitors Bureau; p. 5 USDA photo by Scott Bauer; pp. 6, 9
© North Wind Picture Archives; p. 11 © ArtToday; pp. 12, 16, 21, 22, 25,
28, 29 Arkansas Dept. of Parks & Tourism; p. 18 © PhotoDisc

Printed in the United States of America

1 2 3 4 5 6 7 8 9 10 09 08 07 06

CONTENTS

★ ★

Words that are defined in the Glossary appear
in **bold** the first time they are used in the text.

On the Cover: The Buffalo River makes its way through the high cliffs,
tree-lined banks, and clear waters of Arkansas's Ozark Mountains.

Introduction

If you could visit Arkansas, what would you like to see? The Ozark Mountains? Bean Cave? Hot Springs? The Crater of Diamonds?

Arkansas has great natural beauty. The state has forests and mountains, clear lakes and rivers, and dazzling waterfalls. It has tall, flowering trees and colorful wildflowers. The way of life there is an exciting blend of old and new, country and city.

The people of Arkansas are proud of their state's beauty. They invite visitors to experience the wonders of their state.

Welcome to Arkansas!

Bathhouse Row in Hot Springs National Park is a part of Arkansas's history. Many visitors once came here to bathe in the warm waters.

The state flag of Arkansas.

ARKANSAS FACTS

- Became the 25th U.S. State: June 15, 1836
- Population (2004): 2,752,629
- Capital: Little Rock
- Biggest cities: Little Rock, Fort Smith, North Little Rock, Fayetteville
- Size: 52,068 square miles (134,856 square kilometers)
- Nickname: The Natural State
- State Tree: Southern pine
- State Flower: Apple blossom
- State Mammal: White-tailed deer
- State Bird: Mockingbird

History

People have lived in Arkansas for more than ten thousand years. Early Native groups used spears to hunt large animals. Later groups farmed the land. They grew corn, squash, beans, and other crops. Some of the people built large mounds made of earth. Sometimes, they buried people in the mounds. Other mounds had special buildings for ceremonies.

Explorers and Settlers

Hernando de Soto was an explorer from Spain. He reached the Arkansas region in 1541. De Soto hoped to find gold in the New World. He found rich land, but he never found gold.

In 1682, Robert de La Salle came to the area. He was a French explorer. La Salle

The Plum Bayou people built mounds of earth hundreds of years ago. Some of these mounds were used for special ceremonies.

Early Burial Ground

In 1974, workers found a small burial site in northeastern Arkansas. They called it the Sloan Site. The site was named after the people who owned the land. Workers found bones and many stone points here. The points had been used at the end of spears. The site is about 10,500 years old. It is the oldest known cemetery in North America.

claimed the entire region around the Mississippi River for his country. The land that later became Arkansas was part of this big region. La Salle named the land he had claimed *Louisiana* after Louis XIV. Louis was the king of France.

In 1686, a Frenchman named Henri de Tonti returned to the Arkansas area. He had been there before with Robert La Salle. De Tonti founded a trading post. It was the first white settlement in the region. He named it the Arkansas Post. Henri de Tonti is known as the father of Arkansas.

In 1763, France gave the Louisiana Territory to Spain. This was part of a **treaty** to end a war. France bought the land back from Spain in 1800.

White settlers started to move to the Arkansas area in the late eighteenth century. In 1803, France sold the Louisiana Territory to the United States.

Territory and Statehood

The Arkansas Territory was set up in 1819. Over the next several years, thousands of settlers moved to the area. On June 15, 1836, Arkansas became the twenty-fifth state to join the United States.

FACTS

Native Name

The name *Arkansas* comes from a Native word. The Quapaw people of the area were called the *Akansea* or *Arkansas* by other Natives. These names mean "people of the south wind."

Most of the Natives in the state were forced to move from their land and homes. They had to live in a place farther west.

Civil War

By the mid-1800s, the nation was divided over the issue of slavery. Many people in the Southern states had slaves. Most people in the North did not. They thought slavery was wrong. People in Arkansas were divided, too. Many farmers owned slaves, but others did not.

IN ARKANSAS'S HISTORY

Emerald City?

In 1722, a French explorer named Bernard de La Harpe searched for a giant green rock in the Arkansas area. The Quapaw people had told La Harpe about this rock. He hoped it would be a giant emerald. La Harpe found a big rock on the shore of the Arkansas River. A short distance away, he also found a smaller rock. Neither rock was an emerald. They were river markers to help travelers find their way. La Harpe built a trading post near the smaller rock. He named the trading post *Little Rock*. Today, the city of Little Rock is the state capital.

The Southern states began to **secede**, or pull out of the **Union**. They formed their own country. They named it the Confederate States of America. The people of Arkansas called a special meeting. They decided to support the Union. One month later, they met again. This time, they voted to secede. The state soon joined the Confederacy.

The Civil War began in 1861. The North fought the South. Some of Arkansas's soldiers fought on the side of the North. Others fought for the South.

More than fifteen battles were fought in the state. A major battle took place at Pea Ridge in 1862. The North won the battle. The next year, Union troops captured Little Rock.

Dark Times

The Union won the war in 1865. Three years later, Arkansas became part of the Union again. After the war, all slaves in the state were freed. Even so, they did not have the same rights as most white people. Poor whites did not have equal rights, either.

The Battle of Pea Ridge took place near Elkhorn Tavern in 1862 during the Civil War. Northern forces won this battle.

IN ARKANSAS'S HISTORY

Battle Names

Soldiers from the North and South fought at Pea Ridge during the Civil War. This battle had two names. Northern troops named it the Battle of Pea Ridge. Pea Ridge was the name of the hill where the fighting took place. Southern troops called it the Battle of Elkhorn Tavern. They named battles after the nearest buildings.

Famous People of Arkansas

Scipio Africanus Jones

Born: c. 1863, Tulip, Arkansas

Died: March 2, 1943, Little Rock, Arkansas

Scipio Africanus Jones was born a slave. After the Civil War, he went to black schools close to his home. Jones wanted to be a lawyer, but the University of Arkansas would not accept black students. Jones studied law on his own. He passed the state exam and became a lawyer. Jones wanted to help African Americans who needed a fair trial. His most famous case was defending twelve men who had been found guilty of murder. Jones asked for a new trial. The case went to the U.S. Supreme Court. The new trial proved the men did not get a fair trial the first time. Six of the men were released right away. The other six were sent back to jail. The governor later pardoned these men.

Railroads came to Arkansas after the Civil War. They made jobs for people in the state. Railroads also meant a new way to move crops and goods to many places. Travel became easier for those who could afford to ride the trains. This growth continued into the next century.

A New Century

World War I and World War II were fought in the first half of the twentieth century. Both of these wars took place overseas. Soldiers from all the states in the nation fought in these wars.

Floods and **drought** in the new century brought some

hard times to the people of Arkansas. Also, the **Great Depression** began in the early 1930s. During this time, the prices people paid for goods fell. Workers lost their jobs. A government program called the New Deal gave some people work to do in the state.

Slavery had ended with the Civil War. Even so, not all people in the nation had equal rights. In 1957, a U.S. court said Central High School in Little Rock must accept black students. Only white students went to this school. The governor would not follow the court's order. U.S. president Dwight Eisenhower sent the U.S. Army to Little Rock. The troops made sure African American students were allowed into the school. This event was a turning point in the country's fight for civil rights.

Many people from Arkansas helped build railroads after the Civil War.

Bill Clinton, who was born in the town of Hope, became the forty-second U.S. president in 1993. Before that, he had been governor of Arkansas for five terms. Clinton was reelected to the presidency in 1996.

Today in Arkansas

In 2004, former president Bill Clinton opened the new Clinton Presidential Center and Park in Little Rock. The center has a museum and library. It also has a School of Public Service.

FUN FACTS

Positive Role Model

Hillary Rodham Clinton has spent many years in public life. She is the wife of former U.S. president Bill Clinton. She was First Lady of Arkansas for ten years. She was First Lady of the country for eight years. Then, she became a U.S. senator from New York. She works hard to reach her goals. Hillary Rodham Clinton sets a good example for girls everywhere.

The main library of the Clinton Presidential Center stretches out over the waters of the Arkansas River.

1541	Spanish explorer Hernando de Soto lands in the Arkansas area.
1682	French explorer Robert de La Salle claims the entire region around the Mississippi River for his country. This includes the Arkansas region. He names the land *Louisiana*.
1803	France sells the Louisiana Territory to the United States. It is called the Louisiana Purchase.
1819	The Arkansas Territory is formed.
1836	Arkansas becomes the twenty-fifth state in the Union on June 15.
1861–1865	The North fights the South in the Civil War. In 1862, the Battle of Pea Ridge is fought in Arkansas.
1917–1918	Soldiers from Arkansas fight alongside other U.S. troops in World War I.
1930s	The Great Depression causes hardship in Arkansas and all other U.S. states.
1941–1945	Arkansas sends soldiers to fight in World War II.
1957	President Dwight Eisenhower sends the U.S. Army to **escort** African American students to school in Little Rock.
1993	William Jefferson Clinton from Hope, Arkansas, becomes the forty-second president of the United States.
1996	Bill Clinton is reelected to a second term as president of the United States.
2004	The Clinton Presidential Center and Park is dedicated in Little Rock.

People

rkansas has 2.7 million people. The population is growing. Some people are moving to the state because of the mild climate. Others want to enjoy the beautiful scenery. Prices for homes are lower than in some other areas of the country. It does not cost quite as much to live in Arkansas.

People are moving to all parts of the state. The northwestern part of the state offers many jobs. Some big companies, such as Wal-Mart and Tyson Foods, have

Hispanics: In the 2000 U.S. Census, 3.2 percent of the people living in Arkansas called themselves Latino or Hispanic. Most of them or their relatives came from places where Spanish is spoken. They may come from different racial backgrounds.

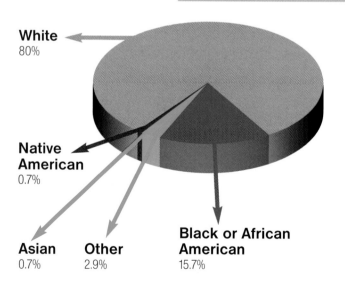

The People of Arkansas

Total Population 2,752,629

White
80%

Native American
0.7%

Asian
0.7%

Other
2.9%

Black or African American
15.7%

Percentages are based on the 2000 Census.

their main offices in this part of Arkansas.

Arkansas is a **rural** state. Almost half of the people live in the country or in small towns. Farming, mining, and forestry still offer good ways for people to make a living.

For thousands of years, Native Americans have lived on this land. Today, the Native population is quite small. The state is home to fewer than twenty thousand Native people.

The first settlers came mostly from other states in the South. Some brought slaves with them. Before the Civil War, about one-fourth of the state population was black. Although many

Old Main is the oldest building at the University of Arkansas-Fayetteville. It was built in 1875. In 1970, it was added to the National Register of Historic Places.

Workers from Mexico and Central America are leaving their homes to move north. They want to find good jobs in the United States.

Education and Religion

The state did not have many schools in its early days. Education became more important after the Civil War, however. A state board of education formed in 1909. Its job still is to improve the quality of education. Today, about 35 percent of the state budget is used for education.

African Americans left the state during the Great Depression, they now are moving back. Some cities in the state today are more than 50 percent black.

Many Hispanic people also are moving to the state.

Famous People of Arkansas

Hattie Wyatt Caraway

Born: February 1, 1878, Bakerville, Tennessee

Died: December 22, 1950, Falls Church, Virginia

Hattie Wyatt went to college in the 1890s, when she was eighteen years old. At that time, most women did not go to college. Instead, they stayed at home. She became a teacher. She married Thaddeus H. Caraway. He was elected to the U.S. House of Representatives from Arkansas. Later, he was elected to the U.S. Senate. Senator Caraway died in 1931. He was still in office. Hattie took his place for the rest of his term. At election time, she ran for the Senate from Arkansas and won. Hattie Caraway was the first woman ever elected to the U.S. Senate. She served until 1945.

Arkansas now has eleven public universities. It also has twenty two-year public colleges. The University of Arkansas is the largest public university system in the state. It opened in 1871. Arkansas has at least twelve private schools of higher learning, too.

About 90 percent of the people in Arkansas are Christians. Many of them are Protestants. More than 40 percent of the people are Baptists. Others are Methodists, Lutherans, and Episcopalians. Some Jews, Buddhists, and Muslims also live in the state.

The Land

The state has two main regions. The highlands, or uplands, are in the northwestern part of the state. This area is home to the Ozark Mountains. It is a land of tall **summits**, deep **gorges**, and rushing waterfalls.

The Ouachita Mountains are just south of the Ozarks. Both areas have warm, underground springs. These springs bubble up to the surface. The area has many resorts. Visitors bathe in the hot springs. People believe the warm waters are healthy.

Magazine Mountain is the highest point in the state. It lies between the Ozark and Ouachita Mountains. It rises 2,753 feet (839 meters) above sea level.

The lowland region is in the southeastern part of the state. The wet lowlands are flat. They also are rich for farming. Part of this area once was the coast of the Gulf of Mexico. But the coast has moved south over millions of years. Another rich farming area is the Arkansas River

FUN FACTS

Finders Keepers!

A farmer near Murfreesboro found diamonds on his land in 1906. The land now is the Crater of Diamonds State Park. It is one of the largest diamond fields in the world. People can visit the park and dig for diamonds there. If they find one, they can keep it. Many visitors also find other gems and rocks in the park. The diamond is the official state gem.

ARKANSAS

MISSOURI

Hot Pea Ridge NMP

Rogers

Beaver L.

Bull Shoals L.

Black R.

Springdale

O Z A R K

Buffalo R.

Paragould

Fayetteville

M O U N T A I N S

White R.

Blytheville

Jonesboro

Mountain View

B O S T O N

Greers Ferry L.

M O U N T A I N S

Van Buren

Alma

L. Dardanelle

Fort Smith

Russellville

Arkansas R.

Searcy

West Memphis

Conway

Magazine Mt.

Forrest City

L. Ouachita

Little Rock

North Little Rock

O U A C H I T A

M O U N T A I N S

W. Helena

Hot Springs NP

Stuttgart

White R.

Malvern

Arkadelphia

Pine Bluff

Arkansas R.

Mississippi R.

Murfreesboro

Crater of
Diamonds SP

Millwood L.

Ouachita R.

Saline R.

MISSISSIPPI

Hope

Red R.

Camden

Texarkana

Magnolia

El Dorado

OKLAHOMA

TENNESSEE

St. Francis R.

TEXAS

LOUISIANA

N
W   E
S

SCALE/KEY

0	50 Miles

0	50 Kilometers

⊛ State Capital

▲ Highest Point

▨ Mountains

19

FUN FACTS

Sounds of Music

A dulcimer is a musical instrument. When Scots and Irish settlers moved to America, they missed the sound of their home music. Some began to make their own dulcimers. They became known as mountain dulcimers. These are long, wooden box instruments. Each one has three or four strings to pluck or strum. Craft workers in Mountain View make dulcimers. This city is in the Ozark Mountains. Dulcimers play an important part in the local folk music.

Major Rivers

Mississippi River
2,357 miles (3,792 km) long

Arkansas River
1,450 miles (2,333 km) long

White River
690 miles (1,110 km) long

provides a good climate for visitors and the people who live there. Sometimes, the state has tornadoes and strong thunderstorms. These usually occur in the low river valley areas.

Waterways

Arkansas has lots of water. It has many beautiful lakes. The state also has more miles of usable rivers than most other states. The Mississippi River runs along the eastern side of the state. All this water is good for moving goods from one place to another. It also

Valley. It lies between the Ozark and Ouachita Mountains.

Climate

The state has four seasons. Each one is fairly mild. This

gives people plenty of room for water sports. The scenic Buffalo River is special. In 1972, Congress named it a national river. This means people cannot build a **dam** on the river.

Plants and Animals

About half of the state is forest. Many types of trees grow there. Oak, hickory, and sugar maples grow in the north. Cypress, pecan, and pines grow in the south. The southern pine is the state tree. Many flowering trees and shrubs, as well as colorful native flowers, add to the natural beauty.

Arkansas has ten national wildlife refuges. Animals can roam free in the thick forests. Black bears, bobcats, deer, alligators, and beavers are only a few of the native wildlife. The white-tailed deer is the state mammal. Great blue herons, red-tailed hawks, and vultures are a few of the many birds in the area. The mockingbird is the state bird. Many types of snakes also live in the state. Walleye, bass, and trout thrive in the state's many lakes and streams.

Clear, clean Lake Ouachita is a perfect place for camping and water sports. It covers 40,000 acres. Lake Ouachita National Forest surrounds the lake.

CHAPTER 5

Economy

A rkansas has many natural resources. These resources help provide jobs for the people who live there. The state's main resources are oil, natural gas, and **bromine**. Bromine is a chemical. It is used in gasoline and dyes. The state also has hot springs and diamonds.

Forests in the state make lumber for the building industry. Some big companies have their own tree farms. These farms grow pine and other types of trees.

Farming

Arkansas has about fifty thousand farms. The state has a mild climate. It also has

Large machines help harvest crops on Arkansas farms. Farming is still big business in the state.

plenty of water and rich soil. Crops can grow for many months each year. Arkansas produces more rice than any other state in the country. Other major farm crops are soybeans, broiler chickens, catfish, cotton, and wheat.

Making Goods

People in the state began making goods to sell during World War II. This gave jobs to many people. Today, workers make paper and furniture. They also make machines, car and airplane parts, steel, and plastics.

Tourism

Arkansas's natural beauty attracts many tourists each year. It is a fun place for anyone who likes to be outdoors. People who visit the state also spend money there. Their money helps the **economy**.

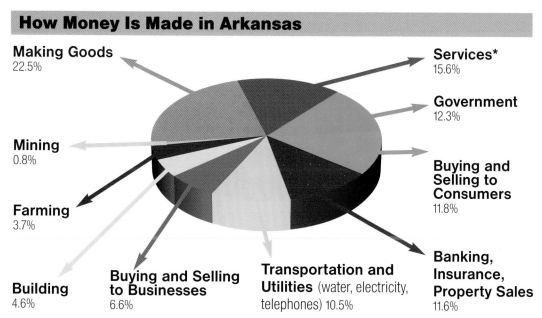

How Money Is Made in Arkansas

Making Goods 22.5%

Mining 0.8%

Farming 3.7%

Building 4.6%

Buying and Selling to Businesses 6.6%

Transportation and Utilities (water, electricity, telephones) 10.5%

Services* 15.6%

Government 12.3%

Buying and Selling to Consumers 11.8%

Banking, Insurance, Property Sales 11.6%

* Services include jobs in hotels, restaurants, auto repair, medicine, teaching, and entertainment.

Government

Little Rock is Arkansas's capital city. The state's lawmakers work there. The government has three parts. These parts are the executive, legislative, and judicial branches.

Executive Branch

The governor is head of the executive branch. This branch makes sure state laws are carried out. The lieutenant governor and other officials help the governor.

The Arkansas state capitol in Little Rock is almost one hundred years old. It looks like the U.S. capitol in Washington, D.C.

The governor's mansion was built in Little Rock in 1950.

Legislative Branch

The legislative branch makes laws for the state. The legislature, which is called the General Assembly, has two bodies. It has a Senate and a House of Representatives. The Senate and House work together.

Judicial Branch

Judges and courts make up the judicial branch. Judges and courts may decide whether people who have been accused of committing crimes are guilty.

Local Government

Arkansas is divided into seventy-five counties. The highest official in each county is a county court judge. County court judges are elected to serve terms of four years.

ARKANSAS'S STATE GOVERNMENT

Executive		Legislative		Judicial	
Office	**Length of Term**	**Body**	**Length of Term**	**Court**	**Length of Term**
Governor	4 years	Senate		Supreme (7 justices)	8 years
Lieutenant Governor	4 Years	(35 members)	4 years	Appeals (12 judges)	8 years
		House of Representatives			
		(100 members)	2 years		

Things to See and Do

Arkansas is a state of the great outdoors. Its natural beauty is awesome. There are many exciting places to see and fun things to do.

Outdoor Paradise

Arkansas has six national parks. It also has fifty-one state parks. Hot Springs National Park was the first national park in the country. It has a famous resort. The city of Hot Springs has rows of bathhouses. Many people believe the hot water is healthy. The resort has horse

Civil War Cave

Eastern Arkansas has many caves. Bean Cave played a big role in the Civil War. The cave had a type of rock salt in its clay walls. This rock salt was mixed with charcoal and **sulfur** to make gunpowder. As many as one hundred men worked in Bean Cave to make gunpowder for the Southern soldiers. Eventually, Union troops destroyed the cave.

Petit Jean State Park is one of more than fifty state parks in Arkansas.

Blanchard Springs Caverns are full of amazing sights. These caverns are located near Mountain View.

Johnny Cash

Born: February 26, 1932, Kingsland, Arkansas

Died: September 12, 2003, Nashville, Tennessee

Johnny Cash was a country music star. He learned to play the guitar as a young boy. He moved to Memphis, Tennessee, in the 1950s. He wanted to play music for a living. It did not take him long to become a success. He had a deep, powerful voice. Also, he wrote songs about the many challenges of life. "I Walk the Line" and "Ring of Fire" were two of Cash's most popular songs. He always wore black. He said this was to show that he cared about all the people who suffered in the world. Johnny Cash was voted into the Country Music Hall of Fame in 1980. He was voted into the Rock and Roll Hall of Fame in 1992.

racing, theme parks, musical shows, and places to shop.

Visitors also can explore the state's caves and caverns. Blanchard Springs Caverns is open all year round. This huge **limestone** cave system is in the Ozark National Forest. One of the rooms is as large as six football fields!

Festivals

The Armadillo Festival takes place in Hamburg each year.

Famous People of Arkansas

Sam Walton

Born: March 29, 1918, Kingfisher, Oklahoma

Born: April 5, 1992, Little Rock, Arkansas

Sam Walton was a well-known businessman. He opened the first Wal-Mart **discount** store in Rogers, Arkansas, in 1962. Thirty years later, the country had seventeen hundred stores. Walton sold goods at low prices. This way, people could buy more. And he could make more money. Sam Walton was successful. He became one of the richest men in the country.

The Arkansas Air Museum is history in action. Although the aircraft are antiques, many of them still fly.

Paris has the Mt. Magazine International Butterfly Festival. Johnson County has a Peach Festival. There's also a July Fourth rodeo in Springdale. These are only a few of the many exciting events in the state.

Museums and Historic Sites

Arkansas has interesting museums and historic sites. The Arkansas Air Museum in Fayetteville has **vintage** aircraft. Most of the planes still fly. The Ozark Folk Center State Park near Mountain View is a "living" museum. The people who work there show visitors the customs and music of the state's different cultures. The state also has many Civil War sites and Native American mounds. Little Rock now has a special new attraction, too. It is the Clinton Presidential Center. It opened in 2004.

Sports

Arkansas has several minor league sports teams. These include hockey, baseball, and arena football teams. The state does not have any major league teams. The University of Arkansas, however, has many devoted sports fans. Its teams are called the Razorbacks.

Razorback Stadium was built at the University of Arkansas in 1938. Today, it can seat 51,000 football fans.

★ ★

bromine — a chemical element, or basic material, found in nature that is dark red and is used to make dyes and gasoline

dam — barrier built across a waterway to slow down water flow

discount — offered for sale at a lower price than usual

drought — a long period of dry weather, with no rain

economy — the system of using money and resources in an organization or state

gorges — deep valleys with steep, rocky sides

Great Depression — a time, in the 1930s, when many people lost jobs and businesses lost money

limestone — a type of rock that is formed mainly by once-living material, such as coral or shells

rural — belonging to the country, or people who live in the countryside

secede — to quit or get out of a group or nation

sulfur — a chemical element, or basic material, found in nature. Sulfur can be used to make gunpowder.

summits — high peaks

treaty — a written agreement

Union — the states that stayed loyal to the federal government during the U.S. Civil War; the North

vintage — belonging to an earlier time; old

Books

Arkansas. Rookie Read-About-Geography (series). Nancy Leber (Children's Press)

Arkansas Facts & Factivities: More Than 100 State Facts That Every Student Needs to Know! Carole Marsh State Books (series). Carole Marsh (Gallopade International)

Maya Angelou. Journey to Freedom (series). Judith E. Harper (Child's World)

N Is for Natural State: An Arkansas Alphabet. Discover America State by State (series). Michael Shoulders (Thomson Gale)

Uniquely Arkansas. Heinemann State Studies (series). Michael B. Dougan (Heinemann Library)

Web Sites

Arkansas Department of Parks and Tourism
www.arkansaskids.com

Arkansas Judiciary Children's Pages
courts.state.ar.us/courts/kids_pages_text.html

Arkansas Online Activity Book
www.sosweb.state.ar.us/education/activity/name.html

Crater of Diamonds State Park, Arkansas
www.craterofdiamondsstatepark.com

National Park Service: Hot Springs, Arkansas
www.nps.gov/hosp/index.htm

INDEX